PRAYER
For
TODAY

An Inspirational Book of Encouragement and Scriptural Prayers

Freda Lade-Ajumobi

PRAYER for TODAY

Copyright © 2013 Freda Lade-Ajumobi

All Rights Reserved

Cover design by Freda Lade-Ajumobi Copyright© 2012

Artwork by Freda Lade-Ajumobi Copyright© 2011, 2012, 2013

All Artwork can be purchased from:

www.freda-ladeajumobi.artistwebsites.com

ISBN-13: 978-1490567754

ISBN-10: 1490567755

DEDICATION

This book is dedicated to Almighty God, the Father, the Son and the Holy Spirit. To God be the glory, great things He has done!

CONTENTS

ACKNOWLEDGMENTS

I would like to acknowledge and express my gratitude for the following people who have had an impact in my life:

I am eternally grateful to our Lord and Saviour, Jesus Christ, who made the impossible possible through His shed blood on Calvary. You are truly awesome!

My darling husband Afolabi, my encourager and my friend, I will forever be grateful to the Lord for you. God bless you.

My son, Timi, you are a gift, a treasure and a blessing. I couldn't wish for a better son. You are an inspiration and a 'God send' to us.

To the happy memory of my father.

My mum, "Mummy Mojola", I am forever grateful for your love and faithfulness. For your endless prayers and for speaking Godly wisdom into my life and ministry. I will forever be grateful to the Lord for you.

My siblings, Pastor Stephen Mojola, Pastor Toyin Lawal and Naomi Adeboye. Thank you for being there. You are a wonderful, loving and supportive family. May God prosper you in all that you do.

Pastor Ida Roy and Patricia MacPepple, for your love, prayers and encouragement over the years. You are both wonderful people.

My church family, City Church Hatfield, for your love. Pastors Mike and Heather Dyce for your faithfulness, love and support. Thank you.

Pastors Kofi and Jayne Banful, you have been instrumental in my foundational walk with the Lord. Thank you.

To Jenny and Melissa Vos, we are no longer friends, we are now family. Thank you Jen for your love, encouragement and support. Love you Mel!

To all my pastor and personal friends, Unique Ministry members and all my encouragers, I am truly grateful. God bless you.

Holy Spirit, my teacher, comforter and friend, thank you!

INTRODUCTION

Have you ever felt low, anxious, depressed and almost given up on life at various moments in your life? Have you been through disappointments and thinking life is not worth living? If like me you have been or are currently going through what I call "walking through the valley" experience, then you are in the right place by taking a look inside this book.

PRAYER for TODAY was written to encourage, uplift and bring healing to others through the power of prayer and the spoken Word of God. It was the power of prayer that pulled me through some very difficult moments in my life and I believe it can do the same for you too.

Through PRAYER for TODAY, I am hoping to give some encouragement and support whilst going through your most difficult and disappointing moments. I am hoping to share the love of God with you, to pray with you and show you how you can speak powerful scriptures that can bring life transforming change into your own life. Like the Apostle Peter said, "Silver and Gold have I none, but what I have give I thee..."

Over the years, I have witnessed how many people

have suffered through depression, disappointments, constant feelings of worthlessness, hopelessness, and despair and have not been able to find the support or help they needed. This is the motivation for writing this book, and I hope you are encouraged by what you read.

It breaks my heart to see people suffer, and initially, I would just get on the phone and give a word of encouragement, but these were only people known to me like friends and family, and then I started writing blogs of encouragement and prayers to uplift more people, as I felt I could reach a wider audience on the Internet. Over the years, I have received lots of emails from my blog readers asking for more, as people felt encouraged and blessed by what they had read.

Prayer and confession of scriptural prayers is a very effective tool of warfare and is what brought me out of darkness into the light that I have come to experience today. There is power in prayer and speaking the Word of God! It worked for me, pulled me out of a dark pit and gave me the strength to face each new day. It gave me hope where once I didn't know where to turn, it brought healing into my life. I know it will work for you. You can use it as a devotional or buy it as a gift for a loved one or for anyone you think would need some encouragement and prayers.

Each prayer is written with you in mind, to inspire, motivate and encourage you to pray. They are to be used by you for yourself and others. Read, meditate and confess the prayers. Praying God's Word brings results, for the Word is of the Sprit of God.

These prayers were written under the inspiration of the Holy Spirit and are based on the Word of God. The Bible states that God watches over His Word to perform it. *"...For I am ready to perform My word." (Jeremiah 1:12)* God's Word released through our tongue will cause His power to manifest in our lives. God will not turn away your prayer; our God hears and answers prayers. He is near to all who call on Him; He is no respecter of persons. He will not despise your prayer. *"Now this is the confidence that we have in Him, that if we ask anything according to His will, He hears us. And if we know that He hears us, whatever we ask, we know that we have the petitions that we have asked of Him." (1 John 5:14-15)* The Lord will hear your supplication and will receive your prayer.

Read PRAYER FOR TODAY and speak the confessions

as often as you can. It can be used as intercessory prayers for others by praying them in the third person. Believe you receive when you pray, God's Word is the key to answered prayer. The Lord is your helper; He will not turn away your prayer.

Most of the prayers have scripture references based on the Word of God. Prayer that brings results must be based on God's Word. ***"For the Word of God is living and powerful, and sharper than any two-edged sword, piercing even to the division of soul and spirit, and of joints and marrow, and is a discerner of the thoughts and intents of the heart." (Hebrews 4:12)*** Prayer is this "living" Word in our mouths. God's Word has creative power. The spoken Word works as we confess it and apply the action to it. These are prayers that bring light and hope.

I pray you are blessed, encouraged, comforted and spiritually lifted as you read the prayers in this book. I pray that your life will be changed and that you will go from faith to faith and from glory to glory. If you are going through hard times, I encourage you to not give up now, there is light at the end of the tunnel. Don't be moved by what you see, for what you see is temporary and subject to change. *"...While we do not look at the things which are seen, but at the things which are not seen. For the things which are seen are temporary, but the things which are not seen are eternal." (2 Corinthians 4:18)*

Don't be moved by adverse circumstances, God will intervene when you use His Word in prayer. We have a God whose eyes are over the righteous and whose ears are open to us; when we pray, He hears us. May the Lord be your Shepherd today and every day, may you not want for any good thing and may God supply all your needs according to His riches in glory in Christ Jesus. God bless you as you commit to prayer and fellowship with Him by using PRAYER for TODAY as a devotional.

MAY GOD ELEVATE YOU

Glory in His holy name;
Let the hearts of those who seek the Lord rejoice!
1 Chronicles 16:10

- May God promote and move you higher. May He reposition and elevate you.

- May He raise your rank. May your status change and His favour locate you.

- May He lift up your spirit and elevate you to a higher dimension.

Zechariah 2:5, **'For I,' says the LORD, "will be a wall of fire all around her, and I will be the glory in her midst."**

I pray that God will be a wall of fire around you and your loved ones. May He be the glory in your midst. I pray that He will be the glory in your home, your family, your marriage, your job and all that concerns you. May you be elevated to a higher place spiritually, mentally and physically and may the favour of God locate you for greater things. No matter what challenges or disappointments you may face in your life, I pray that the Lord will surround you as the mountains surround Jerusalem and may He give you the strength to stand and be victorious in all you do. May God use all the troubles and hardships you may encounter to elevate you and may you soar like an eagle as you embrace the storms of life. When you walk, your steps shall not be hampered, your path will be clear and open; and when you run you shall not stumble.

May God bring you blessings that cannot be quantified. May your blessings overflow and come from all directions, so be expectant because there will be great surprises in store for you. I pray that you will not fall into temptation and all of the devil's strategies to try and lure you into sin will fail and He will not be victorious over you. May the Lord defeat all your enemies. May you cross over to the victorious side and be lifted and elevated in all that you do.

Every mountain and hill before you will be levelled and brought low. All the crooked places in your life will be made straight and the rough places smooth. You shall have the last laugh in Jesus Name. The glory of the

Lord shall be revealed to you and all flesh shall see it together. Concerning you, may the Word of the Lord stand sure forever. When you are weak, may the Lord give you the power to stand and increase your strength. May God contend against those who contend against you and fight against those who fight against you. May He confound and confuse all the plans and strategies of your enemies.

God has chosen you and appointed you to be a ruler in all spheres of life. I pray that you will rule and reign and call those things that are not as though they were. The Lord will build you a house and the sons of wickedness shall oppress you no more. May the Lord subdue all your enemies and make your name great. The Lord will plant you and position you in the right place at the right time in Jesus Name and you shall not fail or fall.

Don't be in a hurry to do things, for the Bible says in Isaiah 28:16, *"... he that believeth shall not make haste."* Be patient and be still before the Lord. Seek His face and ask Him for wisdom in your decision making. I pray that God's wisdom will keep, defend and protect you. As you wait upon the Lord, I pray that God will renew your strength; you shall mount up with wings as eagles, you shall run and not be weary, you shall walk and not faint. Remain blessed and hold steadfastly to His word.

Confession:

- Lord, bless me and keep me. Make your face to shine upon me, and be gracious unto me. Lord, lift up your countenance upon me and give me peace. (Numbers 6:24-26)

- Let all grace abound toward me, that I will have sufficiency in all things and abound to every good work. (2 Corinthians 9:8)

- Lord, strengthen me and bless me with your peace. (Psalm 29:11)

- Let no evil befall me, and no plague come near my dwelling. (Psalm 91:10)

- Let your showers of blessings be upon my life and my family. (Ezekiel 34:26)

- Lord, be a wall of fire around me and be the glory in my midst. (Zech 2:5)

- Let your goodness and mercy follow me all the days of my life. (Psalm 23:6)

- In blessing, bless me, and in multiplying, multiply me as the stars of heaven and as the sand of the seashore.

- Let all the crooked places in my life be made straight and the rough places smooth.

- Let all generations call me blessed. (Luke 1:48)

- Give me your shield of victory and sustain me with your right hand. (Psalm 18:35)

<u>Your verse of the day:</u>

The LORD bless you and keep you;

The LORD make His face shine upon you,

And be gracious to you;

The LORD lift up His countenance upon you,

And give you peace.

(Numbers 6:24-26)

MAY GOD WATCH OVER YOU
AND YOUR FAMILY

He will cover you with His feathers,
And under His wings you will find refuge;
Psalm 91:4

My prayer today is not only for you, but also for your relatives and loved ones. I pray that the love of God will keep and bind you and your family together. I pray that the Lord will pour out His blessings upon your family from on high. Whatever misunderstandings may be in the family, I pray that God will bring His peace to abide in your family. I pray if you have children that God will watch over them and keep them safe, and if you have brothers and sisters that God's grace will abound towards them. I pray that there will be no loss of life in your family. I pray that your family dwells in a peaceable habitation, in safe dwellings and in quiet resting places. I pray that you and your family will always be at the right place at the right time. I pray that the Lord will command His blessings upon your life. Wherever you go, your steps will be ordered of the Lord. I pray that there will be stability, abundance of salvation, wisdom and knowledge in your home and that God will keep and protect your entire family from evil. He will keep you from all harm. If there is any sick person in your family, I pray that the healing hand of God will reach out and touch the one who is sick. I pray that God's power will envelope him/her and bring the healing that is needed. I pray that God will surround you and your family with His love. May the Lord be gracious to you, may He be your strength and defence. May His favour surround you forever and may His peace continually be your guide today and always. Keep the peace of God in your heart and it shall be well with you. Amen.

Confession:

- Lord, bless my family and my home. (Proverbs 3:33)

- Surround my family with your favour as with a shield. (Psalm 5:12)

- Be our strong tower from the enemy. (Psalm 61:3)

- Surround my family with your love and keep us under the shadow of your wings.

- Lord, make my family to dwell in safety. (Psalm 4:8)

- Keep and protect us from evil.

- Let there be no loss of life in my family.

- Cover us with your feathers and be our defence and refuge. (Psalm 91:4)

- Make us to dwell in a peaceful habitation, in secure dwellings and in quiet resting places. (Isaiah 32:18)

- Heal my family and let us enjoy abundant peace and security. (Jeremiah 33:6)

- Lord, deliver my family from strife, discord, division, unforgiveness, anger or ill will in Jesus Name.

- Let your peace be established in my family and my home. (Isaiah 26:12)

- Thank you for establishing peace, unity and harmony into my family.

Your verse of the day:

No evil shall befall you, Nor shall any plague come near your dwelling.

(Psalm 91:10)

MAY GOD DO MIGHTY THINGS FOR YOU

Our mouths were filled with laughter,
Our tongues with songs of joy.
Then it was said among the nations,
"The LORD has done great things for them."
Psalm 126:2

Father in the Name of Jesus I pray for the person reading this book right now. I pray that God will do great and mighty things for you. I pray that you will dance like David danced and sing like David sang. I pray that your joy will be full and there will be no sorrow and weeping in your life. I pray your mouth will be filled with laughter and you will smile again and laugh the last laugh. I pray that whatever may have caused you pain will be removed from your heart and your mourning will turn into dancing again. I pray that the Lord will do great and mighty things for you. I pray that you will look to the Lord for strength at all times. I pray that the God of hope will fill you with all joy and peace as you trust in Him and that you will overflow with hope by the power of the Holy Spirit.

I pray that God will give you the power to get wealth

and that you will use the wealth to help others in their time of need. I pray that those who have despised you will in turn come back and honour you. I pray that God will make your enemies to be at peace with you and in turn they will become your helper. Your heart will not fail in the Name of Jesus; you will live and not die and proclaim the glory of God. I pray that you will be free from any suicidal or negative thoughts in your mind. I pray that you will come to know your worth and value in life. I pray that you will be content with who you are and that you will be able to love others as yourself. Finally, I pray that it shall be well with you, your family, your children, your husband, your wife and all those that you love. God bless you for reading this prayer.

Confession:

- Lord, do great and mighty things for me.

- Fill me with hope, joy and peace.

- Keep my heart from failing and fill me with your everlasting joy.

- I apply the blood of Jesus between me and the spirits that torment me.

- Lord, deliver me from all my troubles and do mighty things for me. (Psalm 34:17)

- My hope is in you; let me never be put to shame. (Psalm 25:3)

- Heal my heart and bind up my wounds. (Psalm 147:3)

- Even though I walk through the valley of the shadow of death I will fear no evil. (Psalm 23:4)

- Let my soul be filled with all joy and peace as I put my trust in you.

- Let your joy be my strength. (Nehemiah 8:10)

- Lord, make my enemies to be at peace with me. (Proverbs 16:7)

- Multiply me and increase my joy. (Isaiah 9:3)

- Lord, thank you for doing great and mighty things for me. (Luke 1:49)

Your verse of the day:

For He who is mighty has done great things for me, And holy is His name.

(Luke 1:49)

MAY GOD BLESS YOU AND KEEP YOU

Cast all your anxiety on Him
Because He cares for you.
1Peter 5:7

Today, I pray that you shall prosper and be in health, even as your soul prospers. I pray that the Lord will bless you and anoint you with fresh oil. I pray that you will flourish like a palm tree and grow like a cedar in Lebanon. I pray that the Lord shall give His angels charge over you to keep you in all your ways. I pray that God will look after you and your family. As no family is perfect, may the love of God bind you and your family together. May God's strength be made perfect in your weakness. If you feel your family don't care and you've been ignored and left lonely, may God raise people up who will be like a family and a pillar to you and may you find comfort in the love of friends. If you are offended by some kind of abuse or lack of love given to you by your family, if there are disputes within your family that you are not able to resolve, I pray that you will be able to give this burden over to God and let Him intervene on your behalf.

I pray that today will be the beginning of a healing process for you. I pray that God will heal you, make you whole and reconcile you with your family. May the Lord plant a hedge of protection around you, may He bless you and keep you, may He cause his face to shine upon you and give you peace in Jesus Name. Amen.

Confession:

- Lord, bless me and strengthen me by your might and power.

- Bless me indeed, and enlarge my coast, let your hand be with me, and keep me from evil. (1 Chronicles 4:10)

- Protect me and my family and show us your mercy and kindness. (Numbers 6:24)

- Keep us from all harm and watch over our lives.

- Watch over our coming and going both now and forevermore. (Psalm 121:8)

- Let your angels ascend and descend upon our lives. (Genesis 28:12)

- Lord, be present in my family and my home. Fill each one of us with your love and understanding.

- Unite us with your cord of love and help us to forgive one another.

- I break the power of all negative words spoken against me and my family.

- Let your healing waters flow into my life and make me whole.

- Lord, give me peace always by all means, and be with me. (2 Thessalonians 3:16)

- Restore peace and unity in my home.

- Let me know the love of Christ, which passes all understanding, that I might be filled with all the fullness of God. (Ephesians 3:19)

- Let me stand perfect and complete in all the will of God. (Colossians 4:12)

- Lord, let your glory be declared among my family and your wonders in my nation. (Psalm 96:3)

- I shall flourish like a palm tree and grow like a cedar in Lebanon. (Psalm 92:12)

<u>Your verse of the day:</u>

"For I know the thoughts that I think toward you,

says the LORD,

Thoughts of peace and not of evil,

To give you a future and a hope."

(Jeremiah 29:11)

MAY GOD PROTECT YOU

I pray the Lord will bless you and protect you,
And that He will show you mercy and kindness.
May He be good to you
And grant you peace.

My prayer for you today is a prayer of protection. I pray that God will protect and keep you safe. Because you have made the Lord your refuge, even the Most High, your dwelling place, no evil shall befall you nor shall any disease, disaster or plague come near your dwelling place. Because you have made the Most High your dwelling place, your family will be safe, your children will be safe, your marriage will be safe, your husband will be safe, your wife will be safe, your job will be safe. If you are single you will marry, if you are married your marriage will not break down in Jesus Name. You will be happy and joyful. You will be promoted and find favour in the sight of God and man. No sudden calamity will come against your household. The Lord shall give His angels charge over you, to keep you in all your ways. In their hands they shall bear you up, in case you dash your foot against a stone. I pray that you will know and be grateful that God watches over you night and day. He will never leave nor forsake you. I pray His shadow will never depart from you.

May the Lord bring you out of trouble and set you in a safe place. You will call upon the Lord and He will answer you. He will be with you in trouble; He will deliver you and honour you. May the Lord give you long life and satisfy you with good things. I pray that you will be full of life and strength. When worry is great within you, may God bring comfort and joy to your soul. The Lord will be a strong place for you, He will be your High tower and you will run into Him and be safe. He will be your Rock and hiding place now and forevermore. Amen.

Confession:

- Lord, cover my head in the day of battle. (Psalm 140:7)

- Let me lie down and rest in safety. (Job 11:18)

- Let your glory be my covering and protect my back.

- Be my refuge and my fortress. (Psalm 91:2)

- Let no evil befall me nor any disease, disaster or plague come near my dwelling place. (Psalm 91:10)

- I shall not be afraid of the terror by night, or of the arrow that flies by day. (Psalm 91:5)

- Lord, you are my keeper. Be my shade and preserve me from all evil. (Psalm 121:5, 7)

- Be my Rock and my hiding place.

- Bring me out of trouble and set me in a safe place.

- Give me long life and satisfy me with good things.

- Lord, protect me, my family, and my home and perfect all that concerns me.

- Preserve my going out and my coming in now and forevermore. (Psalm 121:8)

<u>Your verse of the day:</u>

Surely He shall deliver you from the snare

of the fowler,

And from the perilous pestilence.

He shall cover you with His feathers,

And under His wings you shall take refuge.

(Psalm 91:3-4)

MAY GOD BLESS YOU TODAY

The Lord will keep you from all harm;
He will watch over your life;
The Lord will watch over your coming and going
Both now and forevermore.
Psalm 121:7-8

May God bless you today and keep you always.

May all your enemies be confounded and put to

shame.

May you be the head and not the tail.

May you arise and shine.

May you shine and be enriched.

May the One who neither sleeps nor slumber watch

over you.

May you know today that you are beautiful,

You are not ugly, and nothing is ugly

Because God the creator is beautiful.

May you blossom like a flower,

May you prosper and be in good health.

May your soul prosper.

May you never lack any good thing.

May you never beg for bread or want for any good

thing.

May all that you lay your hands to do prosper.

May today be the beginning of a new chapter

for you and all that you love.

Remain blessed. Amen.

<u>Confession:</u>

- Lord, bless me today and every day.

- Let me prosper and be in good health.

- Let all my enemies be confounded and put to shame.

- Let your showers of blessings be upon my life. (Ezekiel 34:26)

- Let your blessings make me rich. (Proverbs 10:22)

- I am the head and not the tail. (Deut 28:13)

- I am above only and not beneath. (Deut 28:13)

- No weapon formed against me shall prosper. (Isaiah 54:17)

- I shall prosper and be in good health. (3 John1:2)

- I shall not lack any good thing in Jesus Name.

<u>Your verse of the day:</u>

You anoint my head with oil; my cup runs over.

Goodness and mercy shall follow me

All the days of my life.

(Psalm 23:5-6)

GRACE AND PEACE TO YOU

This then is how you should pray:
"Our Father in heaven, Hallowed be Your name,
Your Kingdom come,
Your will be done on earth, as it is in heaven.
Give us today our daily bread.
Forgive us our debts,
As we also have forgiven our debtors.
And lead us not into temptation,
But deliver us from the evil one.
Matthew 6:9-13

I pray that God will bless you and give you His grace and the strength you need to go through the day. If you had an argument before you left home today, I pray the peace of God will quieten your heart and spirit. I pray you will let go of all resentment, bitterness and strife in any form and that you will give no place to the devil in Jesus name. I pray that you will forgive and release all those who have wronged and hurt you. I pray that the Lord will be your hiding place and that He will preserve you from trouble and give you peace. I pray you will not be confounded and depressed. I pray that the Lord will give you beauty for ashes, the oil of joy for mourning and the garment of praise for the spirit of heaviness. I pray you will not worry or be anxious about anything, but in everything by prayer and petition make your requests known to God. May today be a better day for you than yesterday and may your tomorrows be greater. May the love of God embrace you even now and evermore. Grace and peace to you.

Confession:

- Lord, hallowed be your name. (Luke 11:2)

- Let your grace be sufficient for me. (2 Corinthians 12:9)

- Let your power be made perfect in my weakness. (2 Corinthians 12:9)

- Quieten my heart and my spirit with your peace.

- Let your peace guard and guide my heart in Christ Jesus.

- Let the glory of my latter rain be greater than my former in Jesus Name. (Haggai 2:9)

- Lord, I lift up a standard against any flood the enemy would try to bring into my life. (Isaiah 59:19)

- I bind and cast out any spirit that would try to steal my joy in the name of Jesus.

- Lord, give me wisdom in every area where I lack. (James 1:5)

- Let me be clothed with humility. (1 Peter 5:5)

- Forgive me my trespasses, as I forgive those that have trespassed against me. (Luke 11:4)

- Lead me not into temptation, but deliver me from the evil one. (Luke 11:4)

- I receive abundance of grace and the gift of righteousness, and I reign in life through Christ Jesus. (Romans 5:17)

Your verse of the day:

"Go in peace,

And the God of Israel grant your petition which you have asked of Him."

(1 Samuel 1:17)

YOU SHALL NOT SLIP

He will not let your foot slip,
He who watches over you will not slumber.
Psalm 121:3

Slip - *means to slide, to fall, to slide out of position, to slip from grasp, to lose control, to become worse, to slip into a difficult situation.*

My prayer for you today is that you shall not slip. I pray that the Lord will be your light and your salvation and that you will not fear. The Lord shall be the strength of your life, you shall not be afraid. Though the enemy may strike and lash at you, the Lord will be the stronghold of your life. Though the wicked may come against you to eat up your flesh, your enemies and your foes, they shall stumble and fall. Though an army may encamp against you, your heart shall not fear. Though war may rise against you, in this you will be confident, that in the time of trouble the LORD shall hide you in His pavilion. In the secret place of His tabernacle He shall hide you. The Lord shall set you high upon a rock and your head shall be lifted up above your enemies all around you.

I pray that you will offer sacrifices of joy unto the Lord and that you will sing, yes, you will sing praises to the Lord. The Lord will hear you when you cry with your voice. He will have mercy upon you and answer you. The Lord will not hide His face from you, He will not turn you away in anger, He will be your help and He will not leave you nor forsake you. The Lord will take care of you. He will lead you in a smooth path, because of your enemies who want you to slip. He will not deliver you to the will of your adversaries. All the false witnesses who have risen against you and breathe out violence shall be defeated before you and put to shame. May you see the goodness of the Lord in the land of the living. The Lord of hosts is with you, the God of Jacob is your refuge.

I encourage you today, wait on the LORD; be of good courage, and He will strengthen your heart. Wait, I say on the LORD!

Confession:

- Lord, spread your protection over me and be the stronghold of my life.

- Keep me from all harm and watch over my life.

- Let my foot not slip. (Psalm 121:3)

- Be a wall of fire all around me and my household. (Zechariah 2:5)

- Give your angels charge over me to guard me in all my ways. (Psalm 91:11)

- Let your angels encamp around me to rescue and deliver me from all evil. (Psalm 34:7)

- Deliver me from my enemies and hide me. (Psalm 143:9)

- No weapon formed against me shall prosper, and every tongue that rises against me in judgment I condemn. (Isaiah 54:17)

- I do not have the spirit of fear, but of power and of love and of a sound mind. (2 Timothy 1:7)

- I dwell in the secret place of the Most High, and I abide under the shadow of the Almighty. (Psalm 91:1)

- I have overcome all because greater is He that is in me than he that is in the world. (1 John 4:4)

- I shall not slip in Jesus Name.

Your verse of the day:

The LORD is your keeper;

The LORD is your shade at your right hand.

The sun shall not strike you by day,

Nor the moon by night.

(Psalm 121:5-6)

MAY GOD REMEMBER YOU TODAY

You are my hiding place;
You will protect me from trouble
And surround me with songs of deliverance.
Psalm 32:7

May God remember you today and answer your heart's cries. May He also remember your husband, your wife and your children always. May His joy constantly give you strength. May today be a fruitful and rewarding day for you. I pray that you will have no fear of bad news. I pray that all your heart's desires will be granted and that God will be the glory and the lifter of your head. If you feel low and depressed, I pray that God will strengthen and uphold you as you go through difficult times.

Financially, I pray that God will increase and give you opportunities that will liberate you. May every yoke of oppression and depression be broken from your life. As God remembered Job during his darkest hours, may God remember you and deliver you from all your enemies. May He never leave nor forsake you.

As today is a new day in your life, may all things new begin to happen for you. May God comfort you and increase you on every side. May He make your wilderness like Eden and your desert like a garden. Finally, I pray that God will give you peace in these troubled times and keep your heart from failing. May you obtain joy and gladness and may sorrow and sighing flee away from you today and always. Amen.

Confession:

- Lord, remember me today. (Psalm 106:4)

- Do not forsake me the work of your hands. (Psalm 138:8)

- Remember me and my family and let your joy be our strength.

- Be the glory and the lifter of my head. (Psalm 3:3)

- Strengthen and uphold me in difficult times.

- Lord, part my red sea and make a way for me.

- Deliver me from the yoke of oppression.

- Deliver me from all my enemies.

- Let your showers of blessing be upon my life. (Ezekiel 34:26)

- Let your blessings make me rich. (Proverbs 10:22)

- Make my wilderness like Eden and my desert like a garden. (Isaiah 51:3)

- Let me be satisfied with favour and filled with your blessing. (Deuteronomy 33:23)

- Remember me, O Lord, with the favour that you bring unto your children, and visit me with your salvation. (Psalm 106:4)

Your verse of the day:

When you go to war in your land against the enemy who oppresses you,

Then you shall sound an alarm with the trumpets,

And you will be remembered before

the LORD your God,

And you will be saved from your enemies.

(Numbers 10:9)

MAY TODAY BE THE BEGINNING OF A NEW CHAPTER IN YOR LIFE

For the mountains shall depart
And the hills be removed,
But my kindness shall not depart from you,
Nor shall My covenant of peace be removed,
Says the LORD, who has mercy on you.
Psalm 54:10

Today, I pray that God will give you new ideas and give you opportunities that will open doors for you. I pray that He will lead you to the hidden riches of secret places. I pray that God will give you the wisdom that Solomon had, which made him become the richest man amongst his generation. I pray that your ideas will be unique and unusual. I pray that men will honour you and give you favour in whatever you do and that whatever you lay your hands on shall prosper. I pray that you will not worship the idols of this world, but you will worship the One and only true God. I pray that as you give God time of day, He will bless you and make you prosper. I pray that whatever is like a wall of Jericho in your life will come tumbling down as you put your trust in Him and thank Him for where you are right now. I pray that your hope will never die and that you will find strength in the Joy of the Lord. I pray that those who have despised you will in turn come and honour you.

I pray that people will see you and see the beauty of God in you. I pray that people will appreciate you for who you are and not for what they can get from you. Finally, I pray that the eyes of your understanding will be enlightened so that you can know God better. May today be the beginning of a new chapter in your life and may you find joy and happiness in knowing this, that He who began a good work in you will complete it until the day of Jesus Christ. God bless you today and always. There is light at the end of the tunnel for you and you will rejoice in the end.

Confession:

- Lord, hallowed be your name. (Luke 11:2)

- Let today be the beginning of a new chapter in my life.

- Anoint my head with oil, and let my cup run over. (Psalm 23:5)

Freda Lade-Ajumobi

- Teach me to profit and lead me in the way I should go. (Isaiah 48:17)

- Through your favour I will be a prosperous person. (Genesis 39:2)

- Let your showers of blessings come upon my life. (Ezekiel 34:26)

- Let me see your heaps in my life. (2 Chronicles 31:8)

- Let my vats overflow. (Joel 2:24)

- Let me be a cheerful giver.

- Let my barns be filled with plenty and my presses burst with new wine. (Proverbs 3:10)

- Bring me into a good land without scarceness and lack. (Deuteronomy 8:9)

- Open the floodgates of heaven over my life. (Malachi 3:10)

- Through your favour I will be a prosperous person in Jesus Name. (Genesis 39:2)

<u>Your verse of the day:</u>

"Go in peace,

And the God of Israel grant your petition

which you have asked of Him."

(1 Samuel 1:17)

MAY GOD'S FAVOUR SURROUND YOU

For this reason I kneel before the Father...
I pray that out of His glorious riches
He may strengthen you with power
Through His Spirit in your inner being,
So that Christ may dwell in your hearts through faith.
Ephesians 3:16-17

My prayer for you today is that God will prosper you and favour you. I pray above all things that your soul will prosper and be in good health. I pray as the mountains surround Jerusalem that God will surround you with his favour. I pray that when you go for any interviews or meetings that God will give you favour in the sight of men. I pray that God will put His words in your mouth and that you will prosper and be successful in all that you do. I pray that He will energize you to achieve more for yourself so that you can empower others. I pray that God's hand of mercy and faithfulness will not depart from you and your family. I pray that the Almighty will transform your life and all your disappointments will turn into joy. Your mourning will be turned into dancing again. God will visit you and meet you at your point of need and your expectation will not be cut off. You will not be disappointed and whatever may come in the form of disappointments, God will turn it around for your good.

I pray today that you will be the head and not the tail, that you will be above only and not beneath. I pray that all the years that the cankerworm has stolen will be repaid back to you. Your health will spring forth speedily. All your enemies will be disappointed and the Lord will perfect that which concerns you.

My verse for you today is in Isaiah 55:12 and I decree it upon your life: ***"For you shall go out with joy, and be led out with peace; the mountains and the hills shall break forth into singing before you, and all the trees of the field shall clap their hands."***

Rejoice always, again I say rejoice! May the joy of the Lord never depart from you and your household now and forever. Amen.

Confession:

- Lord, strengthen me with your power.

- Prosper and empower me.

- Let your will be done in my life.

- Surround me with your favour.

- Let all my disappointments be turned around for good.

- Energize me to achieve more so I can empower others.

- Let your hand of mercy and faithfulness not depart from me and my family.

- Sanctify me through your Word of truth. (John 17:17)

- Let me be satisfied with favour and filled with your blessing. (Deuteronomy 33:23)

- Let your favour be upon my life as a cloud of the latter rain. (Proverbs 16:15)

- The joy of the Lord is my strength. (Nehemiah 8:10)

Your verse of the day:

And God is able to make all grace abound toward you, that you, always having all sufficiency in all things, may have an abundance for every good work.

(2 Corinthians 9:8)

MAY YOU BE LIKE A CANDLE

Let the light of your life shine in such a way
That others see your good deeds
And bring glory to your Father in heaven.
Matthew 5:16

Today, I pray that you will prosper and be in good health. I pray that your soul will prosper and that you will be strong physically and mentally. I pray that you will be able to avoid the pitfalls of life and make good use of every opportunity. I pray that your life will never be the same again. I pray that you will progress and move forward in life. I pray that God will promote and give you favour at work. I pray that every stagnant situation in your life will become productive and yield good things for you. I pray if you are looking for an answer from God that you will be still and know that He is the God that answers every request according to His will. I pray that your ideas will materialise and bear fruit. I pray that each new venture you put your hand to will prosper. I pray that you will see each difficulty as an opportunity to effect change in your life and in the lives of others.

I pray that you will be like a candle and light up the lives of others. Though you may think your light is small, I pray that you will not underestimate the effect it can have on others when it lights up their lives. I pray that God will cause you to light up other lives and create a revolution of bright lights around the world. I pray that you will make others happy and sow good seeds in life.

May all your prayers yield and manifest good results. May God never leave nor forsake you. May your Angels gather around you and watch over you lest you dash your foot against a stone. May heaven fight all your battles for you and may God provide all your needs according to His riches in glory by Christ Jesus. May you be sufficient and lack nothing today and every day. Peace be unto you.

Confession:

- Lord, lighten my candle and enlighten my darkness. (Psalm 18:28)

- Let your candle shine upon my head. (Job 29:3)

- Let me be a light that will brighten the lives of others.

- Let the mind of Christ be in me and guide me. (Philippians 2:5)

- Let my eyes be enlightened with your Word. (Psalm 19:8)

- Let the righteousness, peace and joy of the kingdom be established in my life. (Romans 14:17)

- Let the fire of your presence be released in my life. (Psalm 97:5)

- Purify my life with your fire. (Malachi 3:2)

- Let me bear fruit and be fresh and flourishing. (Psalm 92:14)

- Let my light so shine that men may see and give glory unto your holy name. (Matthew 5:16)

- My spirit is the candle of the Lord, searching all the inward parts of the belly. (Proverbs 20:27)

- Give me the treasures of darkness and hidden riches in secret places. (Isaiah 45:3)

- Thank you Lord for making my spirit the candle of the Lord.

Your verse of the day:

Then Jesus spoke to them again, saying,

"I am the Light of the world.

He who follows me shall not walk in darkness,

But have the Light of life.

(John 8:12)

MAY YOU BE LIKE A TREE

Blessed is the man who trusts in the Lord,
Whose confidence is in Him.
He will be like a tree planted by the water
That sends out its roots by the stream.
It does not fear when heat comes;

My prayer for you today is that you will be like a tree planted by the waters, which spreads out its roots by the river. I pray that you will not fear when the heat comes, as God will answer you in the time of trouble. May He be your shield and buckler. I pray that like a tree your leaf will remain green, meaning that you will not fade or wither. I pray that you will not be anxious in the year of drought, meaning that you will not be anxious in times of lack, trusting and knowing that God will be your provider. I pray that you will bear fruit in all that you do and that you will not cease yielding fruit. I pray that today will be a rewarding day for you and may all that you do prosper. May you flourish in all that you do and may all your efforts not be in vain. God bless you and your loved ones at all times today and forevermore. Amen.

Confession:

- I shall be like a tree planted by the rivers of water. (Psalm 1:3)

- I shall flourish like a palm tree and grow like a cedar in Lebanon. (Psalm 92:12)

- My life shall bring forth fruit in its season and my leaf also shall not wither. (Psalm 1:3)

- Whatever I do shall prosper. (Psalm 1:3)

- In the time of trouble the Lord shall hide me in His pavilion. (Psalm 27:5)

- He shall hide me in the secret place of His tabernacle. (Psalm 27:5)

- The LORD shall set me high upon a rock. (Psalm 27:5)

- I shall not fear when heat comes or be anxious in the year of drought. (Jeremiah 17:8)

- My head shall be lifted up above my enemies all around me. (Psalm 27:6)

- The LORD is the strength of my life; I shall not fear. (Psalm 27:1)

- I shall flourish in all that I lay my hands to do.

- I shall not cease yielding fruit in Jesus Name. (Jeremiah 17:8)

- Lord, hallowed be your name.

Your verse of the day:

You shall flourish like a palm tree,

You shall grow like a cedar in Lebanon.

(Psalm 92:12)

MAY YOU BE LIKE A CHILD

I will sing to the LORD all my life;
I will sing praise to my God as long as I live.
May my meditation be pleasing to Him,
As I rejoice in the LORD.
Psalm 104:33-34

My prayer for you today is that you will be like a child and forgive others as soon as you are wronged. I pray when your sister or brother, friends, family or colleague wrongs you, you will find the strength to forget like a child would and continue to be at peace with those who have offended you. Like a child, I pray that you will look forward to each new day and forget about the pain of yesterday. I pray that as children trust their parents without doubting their ability that you will put your full and 100% trust in God without doubting His ability to watch over you.

As the presence of a child lightens up a room and brings a smile on people's faces, I pray that your presence will bring smiles on people's faces and brighten up their lives. As a child makes a request of its parents without doubting their ability to provide, I pray that you will not doubt the power of God's provision upon your life.

May you be able to laugh at adversity, knowing this, that He who began a good work in you will complete it in you. May you be the aroma of Christ and always remember to be like a child. It shall be well with you and the Lord will perfect that which concerns you. God bless you today and always.

Confession:

- Let my cry come before you, O LORD. (Psalm 102:1)

- Give me understanding according to your Word. (Psalm 119:169)

- Help me to be quick to forgive others when I am wronged.

- Help me to let go of offence so I can be blessed.

- Lord, deliver me from the snare of the fowler and from the perilous pestilence. (Psalm 91:3)

- Let your presence never depart from me.

- Help me to be like a child and put my trust in you.

- Let me be the aroma of Christ.

- Make me walk in the path of your commandments. (Psalm 119:35)

- Turn away my eyes from looking at worthless things. (Psalm 119:37)

- Let me never doubt your power of provision in my life.

- Accept, I pray, the freewill offerings of my mouth, O LORD, in Jesus Name. (Psalm 119:108)

<u>Your verse of the day:</u>

And those who know your name

will put their trust in you;

For you, LORD, have not forsaken those who seek you.

(Psalm 9:10)

MAY GOD NEVER FORGET YOU

O righteous God,
Who searches minds and hearts,
Bring to an end the violence of the wicked
And make the righteous secure.
Psalm 7:9

In times of adversity, I pray the God of wisdom will remember you. In times of sorrow, I pray the God of joy will comfort you. In times of lack and hardship, I pray that God who owns the cattle on a thousand hills will provide for you. When you walk through the storm, I pray the God of peace will carry you. When all else seems to have failed, I pray the God of hope will strengthen you. When you no longer feel you can continue to carry on, may the eternal Rock of Ages uplift you. Even after you have totally given up, may the God of faithfulness continue to uphold you. I pray that God will perfect that which concerns you and may He never forget you, the work of His hands. May God bless you today and always.

Confession:

- Lord, strengthen me with your power and remember me.

- According to Your mercy remember me. (Psalm 25:7)

- For Your name's sake, O LORD, pardon my iniquity. (Psalm 25:11)

- Lord, bring me out of my distresses. (Psalm 25:17)

- Pluck my feet out of the net. (Psalm 25:15)

- Turn yourself to me, and have mercy on me. (Psalm 25:16)

- For your goodness' sake, O LORD remember me. (Psalm 25:7)

- Do not forsake me the work of your hands. (Psalm 138:8)

- Lord, perfect that which concerns me. (Psalm 138:8)

- To you, O LORD, I lift up my soul. (Psalm 25:1)

- Let me not be ashamed. (Psalm 25:2)

- Let not my enemies triumph over me. (Psalm 25:2)

- Show me your ways, O LORD; teach me your paths. (Psalm 25:4)

- Lead me in your truth and teach me. (Psalm 25:5)

- Keep my soul, and deliver me. (Psalm 25:20)

- Let me not be ashamed, for I put my trust in you. (Psalm 25:20)

Your verse of the day:

"Can a woman forget her nursing child,

And not have compassion on the son of her womb?

Surely they may forget, yet I will not forget you."

(Isaiah 49:15)

MAY YOU HAVE A STRONG MIND

Though I walk in the midst of trouble,
You will revive me;
You will stretch out your hand against the wrath of my enemies
And your right hand will save me.
The Lord will perfect that which concerns me.
Psalm 138:7-8

Today, I pray that your thoughts will line up with God's Word and your mind will not be overcome with negative fleeting or suicidal thoughts. I pray that you will have the willpower to overcome all the negative thoughts that might play on your mind. I pray that you will not give in and agree with the negative thoughts that attack your mind and cause you pain and heartache.

I pray that your mind will be flooded with positive thoughts. I pray that you will believe in yourself, be proud of who you are and know that you are unique and you have been created for a purpose and a reason. I pray you will come to know what your purpose is in life. I pray that you will be content in yourself and know that you are enough as you are. I pray that all those who have put you down will be confounded and in turn they will honour you. God will disappoint all your enemies and give you victory in Jesus Name. I pray that you will be the head and not the tail, that you will be above only and not beneath. I pray that you will know without a doubt that greater is He who is in you than he who is in the world and that those who are with you are more than those that are against you.

I pray that God will bless you abundantly and make you realise that you are worth much more than many sparrows. I pray that your faith will not fail and your expectation will not be cut off. May today bring good news your way and may your prayers be answered. May you and your family be protected from any attacks of the enemy and may God continually be your shield and buckler. I pray that God will bind you and your family together with a cord that cannot be broken. May the love and grace of God abound in your lives and may you learn to sacrifice for each other. Instead of finding faults, I pray that you will encourage one another and forgive any family member who have hurt or let you down. May you have the strength to love again. May God elevate you and your family and bring you to a place of everlasting joy now and forever. Amen.

Confession:

- Lord, give me clarity of vision, clarity of sight, clarity of thought and clarity of mind.

- Lord, wash over my mind with the blood of Jesus.

- Cleanse out all darkness and all thoughts that are contrary to your will and destiny for my life.

- Give me the clarity of knowing and hearing your voice.

- I overcome the devil through the blood of Jesus. (Revelations 12:11)

- Let your power work in me. (Ephesians 3:20)

- Let me be willing in the day of your power. (Psalm 110:3)

- Through the blood of the Lord Jesus Christ, I am redeemed out of the hand of Satan.

- Through the blood of the Lord Jesus Christ, all my sins are forgiven.

- My conscience is purged from dead works to serve the living God through the blood of Jesus. (Hebrews 9:14)

- Through the blood of the Lord Jesus Christ, I am sanctified, made holy and set apart unto God.

<u>Your verse of the day:</u>

For God has not given us a spirit of fear,

But of power and of love and of a sound mind.

(2 Timothy 1:7)

MAY GOD DAILY LOAD YOU WITH BENEFITS AND TURN YOUR DISAPPOINTMENTS INTO JOY

Wait on the LORD;
Be of good courage,
And He shall strengthen your heart;
Wait, I say, on the LORD!

1 Truly my soul silently waits for God; From Him comes my salvation.
2 He only is my rock and my salvation; He is my defence; I shall not be greatly moved. (Psalm 62:1-2)

Today, I pray that your soul will silently wait for God; He is the only one who has the answer to our problems. Perhaps there are questions you want answered and you are looking for satisfaction for your soul. I pray that you will patiently and silently wait upon the Lord for an answer from Him. When you wait on the Lord, you will find comfort for your soul. I pray that God will be your Comforter today and every day. I pray that you will cheerfully give all your affairs to His will and His wisdom. He alone is our Rock and Salvation. I pray that the Lord will be your defence, your deliverer, your shield and buckler. As the mountains surround Jerusalem, may He surround you forever.

If you are worried about your job or anything for that matter, I pray that you will not be greatly moved. I pray that you will wait on God alone and not put your trust in man; for surely the arm of flesh will fail. I pray that God will turn every disappointment around for your good and that you will not cast away your confidence. Though you may feel disappointed by friends and family and your relationships may not work out as desired, I pray that you will find refuge in God and that you will not be moved. I pray that God will daily load you with benefits and turn your disappointments into joy. May God be your salvation and the Rock of your strength. I pray that God will intervene in your case and make all things work together for your good. If you are in pain or have been hurt by loved ones, colleagues or friends, I pray that God will bring healing to your soul and set you free from the pain you are going through. I pray that you will forgive and release those who have hurt you so that your blessings will not be delayed.

The Bible says in Psalm 62: 9-10,

9 *"Men of low degree are a vapour and men of high*

degree are a lie; If they are weighed on the scales, They are altogether lighter than vapour.

10 ...Do not set your heart on them."

God will render to each man according to their works, so do not put your trust in man, only let your soul silently wait on God alone. He alone is able to deliver. It is God that brings out those who are bound into prosperity. I pray that God will bring you into prosperity. I pray that He will give you peace and send you abundance of rain from His goodness.

I pray that God will daily load you with benefits and that your land will produce. He will turn your disappointments into joy and your joy will be full. May your relationships be restored and all that you do prosper now and always. God bless you abundantly now and forever more.

Confession:

- Lord, bless me indeed, and enlarge my coast. Let your hand be with me, and keep me from evil.

- Break off of my life any limitations and restrictions placed on my life by evil spirits in Jesus Name.

- Lord, wash over my mind with the blood of Jesus.

- Bring to me prosperity in my spirit, in my body, in my home, in my finances and in all that I lay my hands to do.

- Lord, bring promotion into my life and make me exceedingly fruitful and blessed.

- I walk in the favour of God and my favour is increased in all that I do.

Your verse of the day:

Have you not known? Have you not heard?

The everlasting God, the LORD, the Creator of the ends of the earth, Neither faints nor is weary.

His understanding is unsearchable.

He gives power to the weak, and those who have no might He increases strength.

Even the youths shall faint and be weary, and the young men shall utterly fall, But those who wait on the LORD shall renew their strength;

They shall mount up with wings like eagles, They shall run and not be weary, They shall walk and not faint. (Isaiah 40:28-31)

MAY GOD ALWAYS BE THERE FOR YOU

I have chosen you...
So that from the rising of the sun to the place of its setting people
may know there is none beside me.
I am the LORD,
There is on other.
Isaiah 45:4-6

Perhaps you are looking for someone to hold your hands and pray with you, or you may be looking for someone to talk to about an issue that is private and you find it difficult to share with anyone else, or you might just be looking for a listening ear, someone to lean on in difficult times, but you find there is no one available in your time of need. Maybe you are feeling alone at this moment in your life.

My prayer for you today is that you will lean on God's everlasting Arms. He is your shelter and your dwelling place. He is big enough to handle all your affairs and deliver you in times of trouble. The Bible says His arms are not too short to save. I want to reassure you today, that as God saved the children of Israel from the hands of the Philistines in the Bible days of old, so will He save you from the hands of all your enemies. I pray that no matter what you might be going through right now, you will put your entire trust in God and He will carry you through.

The Bible says He will keep in perfect peace those whose minds are stayed on Him, because they trust in Him *(Isaiah 26:3)*. Putting your trust in God is key to your victory being made manifest, and so I pray that you will lay down every burden right now, take those bills, put them on a table, lay your hands on them, surrender them to God and pray over the bills, ask God to make a way for you to pay them. Pray over your children, pray for your husband or wife, pray over your job that you will not lose it or if you are looking for a job, pray that God will open doors of favour for you to get one. Pray for God to protect your family from harm, pray that His peace will be your guide, His peace will be your anchor, His peace will bring understanding into your situation and He will make a way out for you. He has done it for me and He can do it for you too. You are His child, the work of His hands.

The Bible says that God saw everything He had made and it was very good *(Genesis 1:31)*. God saw you the work of His hands and it was very good in His eyes. You are unique. You may not look good in the eye of man but in the eyes of God, He sees you as very good. I pray that God's grace will be sufficient for you and that all your disappointments will be turned around for good. Have hope and don't give up because He cares for you.

I pray that Jehovah *Shammah*, the Lord who is always there will continue to be there for you now and forever in Jesus Name. May your home be restored and filled with peace, may your children be blessed and protected by the Spirit of the Lord. He has given His angels charge over you and your family lest you dash your foot against a stone. May you never strike your foot against a stone in Jesus Name.

I pray this year you will not mourn in Jesus Name. Disaster will not come near your dwelling. God will make you and your loved ones dwell in safety and He will watch over you and perfect that which concerns you. May your marriage be blessed, may your family be blessed, may you be satisfied with good things and may you grow more and more in the knowledge of the Lord. Whatever may be broken in your relationships either in your marriage, family or friends, may it be restored back to its former glory in Jesus Name.

I decree peace to you in your home and I break every cord of strife over your life and your family. It shall be well with you and you shall have every reason to rejoice in Jesus Name. You will achieve the unachievable and God will do the impossible for you. You will experience God in a very different and dynamic way and He will reveal a different dimension of Himself to you. May your hunger and thirst for God's righteousness be greater than ever before. I cover you, your family and loved ones with the blood of Jesus and decree that you will always be the head and not the tail in Jesus mighty name. Amen.

Your verse of the day:

"Fear not, for I am with you; be not dismayed, for I am your God. I will strengthen you, yes, I will help you I will uphold you with my righteous right hand."

(Isaiah 41:10)

MAY GOD PROTECT YOU BY THE BLOOD OF JESUS

JESUS SAVES...
For God sent not His Son into the world to condemn the world;
But that the world through Him
Might be saved.
John 3:17

You might be going through a lot at the moment and questioning, "When will it all end?" No one has the answer, as no one apart from God knows the end from the beginning. I cannot guarantee and give you the perfect answer. I don't know when it will all end, but one thing I know is that in spite of it all, Jesus said in His Word that He will never leave nor forsake us if we believe and put our trust in Him. There is power in the Blood of Jesus. No matter what you may be going through right now I pray that the peace of God will surround you and carry you through.

Confession:

I encourage you today to put your trust in Him and confess this prayer:

"Father, in the name of Jesus, I plead the Blood of

Jesus on my entire physical body, on my entire soul and on my entire spirit. I plead the Blood of Jesus on my mind. I plead the Blood of Jesus against any demons that may try and come against me in my home, my family, my finances, my business and in all that I lay my hands to do. I Plead the Blood of Jesus against

any humans that may try and come against me to bully, attack or pull me down. I plead the blood of Jesus against any form of counter attacks sent against me. I cover my family, my home and all my possessions with the blood of Jesus. I cover my job with the blood of Jesus. I cover my finances with the blood of Jesus. I cover my mind and my thoughts with the blood of Jesus. No weapon formed against me shall prosper. Great shall be the peace of my family.

I plead the Blood of Jesus against any natural accidents or catastrophes that may come against me or any member of my family. I plead the Blood of Jesus against any diseases, illnesses or sicknesses that could possibly come against me. I plead the Blood of Jesus against the spirit of discouragement and hopelessness in my life. I shall live and not die; my family shall live and not die and proclaim the glory of God. I shall not mourn in Jesus Name.

Father, in the name of Jesus, I have full faith and I believe that the Blood of Jesus will now protect me against all of the things that I have just Pled His Blood on.

Thank you Father, thank you Jesus for answering my prayers in Jesus Mighty Name I pray". Amen.

<u>Your verse of the day:</u>

"And when I see the blood, I will pass over you;

And the plague shall not be on you to destroy you..."

(Exodus 12:13)

YOU ARE DESTINED TO MAKE IT, YOU WILL NOT FAIL

Therefore put on the whole armour of God,
So that when the day of evil comes,
You may be able to stand your ground,
And after you have done everything,
To stand.
Ephesians 6:13

If someone ever called you a failure, this means that God has destined you for success. If you are feeling tired and weary, the Bible says, *"Let the weak say I am strong." (2 Corinthians 12:10)* If your bills are not adding up, this is an opportunity for you to exercise your faith and believe that Jehovah *Jireh*, our Provider who provides for the birds of the field without them asking for food, will also provide all your needs. If all hell has broken loose on you, this means all heaven is working it together for your good so that you will have an expected and successful end. Without war there is no victory, fix your eyes on victory and hang on to the anchor of hope.

Your victory is in your faith and confession. If you believe that this trial will pass, then it will. Your trial is not forever, it is just another season in your life. This difficult season will definitely pass if you hang on and don't give up. Don't let go, the Bible says after you've done all you know to do, stand therefore *(Ephesians 6:13)*. I encourage you to keep standing even if it seems there is no solution to your problems right now. Hang in there; there is light at the end of the tunnel. This may be your darkest hour; your greatest hour is soon to come. You will rise again. Weeping may endure for a moment, but your joy will come in the morning. God will bring light, peace, solution, answer, provision, love, and all that you need and more your way if you hold on to Him and don't give up. God cares more than we can imagine, but the devil plays on our minds by making us believe God does not answer prayers and that He is not bothered about our pain. He would not have sent His only begotten Son to die for us if this was the case.

If you are feeling down and depressed, there is hope for you, as this is your opportunity to surrender all to God. He is able to carry you through and provide all your needs, but you need to put your trust in Him instead of worrying. Worry will not add anything to your life; it only takes away from you, leaving you with fear and anxiety. This is not your portion. God is able to do exceedingly abundantly above all you can expect or think, so hang in there, surrender all to Him and don't give up. Everything in life is temporary and subject to change, the only thing that never changes is the Word of God, it is the same yesterday, today, and forever. He is the Ancient of Days.

My Word for you today is in Isaiah 26:3-4 (Amplified Bible),

3 You will guard him and keep him in perfect and constant peace whose mind [both its inclination and its character] is stayed on You, because he commits himself to You, leans on You, and hopes confidently in You.

4 So trust in the Lord (commit yourself to Him, lean on Him, hope confidently in Him) forever; for the Lord God is an everlasting Rock [the Rock of Ages].

May God continue to guard and guide you and cause His face to shine upon you and give you peace in these difficult times. Remember to pray for others even as you pray for yourself and God will bless you.

Confession:

- I will flourish like a palm tree and grow like a cedar in Lebanon. (Psalm 92:12)

- I am blessed and highly favoured. (Luke 1:28)

- I can run through a troop and leap over a wall. (Psalm 18:29)

- No weapon formed against me shall prosper. (Isaiah 54:17)

- In everything I do, I am more than a conqueror.

- I am blessed, prosperous and in good health.

- Let me increase in strength and confound the adversaries. (Acts 9:22)

- Let me increase in the knowledge of God. (Colossians 2:19)

- My God shall supply all my needs according to His riches in glory by Christ Jesus. (Philippians 4:19)

- Lord, be a shield for me, my glory and the One who lifts up my head. (Psalm 3:3)

- I am like a tree planted by the rivers of water, I shall not be moved. (Psalm 1:3)

- Lord, make my way prosperous and let me have good success. (Joshua 1:8)

- I will be successful in all that I do; I shall not fail in Jesus name.

<u>Your verse of the day:</u>

God is our refuge and strength,

A very present help in times of trouble.

Therefore we will not fear...

The LORD of hosts is with us;

The God of Jacob is our refuge.

(Psalm 46:1-2, 7)

MAY GOD STRENGTHEN YOU

The Lord gives strength to the weary
And increases the power of the weak.
Isaiah 40:29

God is the great I AM. He is Jehovah *Jireh*, our Provider. I pray that God will provide for you today and every day. He is Jehovah *Shammah*, the Lord who is always there. May the Lord always be there in every moment of your day. He is Jehovah *Shalom*, our Peace. May the peace of God that passes all understanding guard your heart and mind in Christ Jesus. He is Jehovah *Nissi*, our Banner. His banner over you is love. May you come to know and experience the love of God in a very deep and special way. He is Jehovah *Rapha*, our Healer. If you are going through any form of pain or you have sickness in your body, I pray that God will be your Healer. He is Jehovah-*Raah*, our Shepherd. As a shepherd watches over his sheep, may the Lord continually watch over you and protect you from any form of evil. He is *Adonai*, our Master and Jehovah *Mekoddishkem*, the Lord who sanctifies. May the Lord lead you and direct you, may He sanctify you and give you peace in these troubled times.

The Bible mentions God as being *El-Shaddai*, the many breasted One. No matter how many of His children seek Him for help, he will never deny or turn any away. He always listens and hears our cries. I pray at this moment that God will hear all your heart's cries. May He strengthen and encourage your heart and may He be the glory and the lifter up of your head. God is right now listening to those deep things that you find difficult to share with someone else. My prayer is that you will trust Him enough to let go and let Him take those worries from you. He cares for you and will never leave nor forsake you. God is saying to you, *"Trust Me in this, I will not let you down, I will not forsake you"*.

Perhaps things have not been so great lately, maybe a lot has been going wrong in your life and things are probably not working out as you had hoped. I encourage you to take one day at a time; do not take on tomorrow's burdens today. Learn to leave the pain and disappointment of yesterday behind and look forward to a new day. The day has a way of working itself out if only we leave things alone and not worry ourselves thin in trying to make things happen. I encourage you today, why don't you let go and let God? He is able to perfect that which concerns you. Trust in Him and He will carry you through. The pain of today is for the benefit of tomorrow. He is working it all out for your good. No matter how bad things are, there is light at the end of the tunnel. Keep looking forward and moving forward and you will reach where the light is. Don't give up now, God is on your side and He will not let you down. Have hope and it shall be well with you. God bless you today and always. Weeping may endure for a moment, but your joy will come in the morning!

Confession:

- Father keep me from all evil. (John 17:15)

- Sanctify me and give me peace in troubled times.

- Strengthen me in every area of my life.

- Be a hedge of protection over my life.

- I put on the whole armour of God that I might stand in the evil day. (Ephesians 6:13)

- I cancel all the enemies' plans and evil sent against my life in Jesus Name.

- I decree that no evil will touch me in Jesus Name.

- The Lord is the strength of my life. (Psalm 27:1)

- He is my strength and my shield. (Psalm 28:7)

- I am established, anointed and sealed by God in Christ.

- I am covered in the blood of Jesus from the crown of my head to the sole of my feet.

- God's goodness and mercy shall follow me all the days of my life in Jesus name.

Your verse of the day:

My flesh and my heart may fail; but God is the strength of my heart and my portion forever.

(Psalm 73:26)

CALL ON GOD, HE WILL REMEMBER YOU

CALL NOW!
I call on you, O God,
For you will answer me;
Give ear to me
And hear my prayer.
Psalm 17:6

My prayer for you today is that God will answer when you call on Him and He will act on your behalf. I pray that God will remember you even as He remembered Noah and Abraham in the Bible.

In the Bible God remembered Noah...

God remembered Abraham...

God remembered His covenant with Abraham, with Isaac, and with Jacob...

I decree and pray today that God will remember and answer you as He remembered His people in the Bible. In times of distress, God will remember and answer you. In times of depression, I pray that God will remember and answer you. When the tears are flowing and you feel that no one cares, I pray that God who remembered and did not forget to act on behalf of His people will not forget you. When you are searching for an answer and you don't know where to turn, may God come to your aid and answer you.

God will step in on your behalf as you put your faith in Him. May God move in response to your heartfelt cries and prayers and relieve you from your distress. I pray in the same way that God remembered Rachel in the Bible *(Genesis 30:22)* and hearkened to her cry for a child and opened her womb so that she can have a child, may God hearken to your cries and open the windows of heaven's blessings to bless you. May He answer your prayers and hearken to your heart's cries. May God hear your voice and come to your aid. May He answer you and resolve your dilemma and give you peace. No matter what you may be going through right now, I pray that the peace of God that passes all understanding will guard your heart and mind in Christ Jesus. May it be well with you today and forever. Your answer is in Christ Jesus who died for us all. Call on Him today and every day. May God be with you and bless you at all times in Jesus Name. Amen.

Confession:

- Give ear, O Lord, to my prayer; and attend to the voice of my supplications. (Psalm 86:1)

- I call upon you in the day of my trouble, for you will answer me. (Psalm 86:7)

- Be merciful to me, O Lord. For to you, O Lord, I lift up my soul. (Psalm 86:3-4)

- For you are great and do wondrous things. You alone are God. (Psalm 86:10)

- Let my prayer come before you; incline your ear to my cry. (Psalm 88:2)

- Lord, turn to me, and have mercy on me. (Psalm 86:16)

- Show me a sign for good, that those who hate me may see it and be ashamed. (Psalm 86:17)

- Restore me, O God of hosts; cause your face to shine, and I shall be saved. (Psalm 80:7)

- Let me flourish like a palm tree, and grow like a cedar in Lebanon. (Psalm 92:12)

- Let your mercy hold me up and your comforts delight my soul.

- Lord, set me on high because I have known your name. (Psalm 91:14)

- Be with me in trouble; deliver me and honour me. (Psalm 91:15)

- Satisfy me with long life and show me your salvation. (Psalm 91:16)

Your verse of the day:

I will lift up my eyes to the hills,

from whence comes my help?

My help comes from the LORD,

who made heaven and earth.

He will not allow your foot to be moved;

He who keeps you will not slumber.

Behold, He who keeps Israel

shall neither slumber nor sleep.

The LORD is your keeper;

The LORD is your shade at your right hand.

(Psalm 121:1-5)

MAY GOD OPEN NEW DOORS FOR YOU

*REMEMBER the LORD your God,
For it is He who gives you the ability to produce wealth,
And so confirms His covenant,
Which He swore to your forefathers,
As it is today.
Deuteronomy 8:18*

Today, I pray that the God of open doors will open new doors of opportunity for you. I pray that the heavens will open for you and God will pour you out blessings that you will not have room enough to contain it. I pray that no man shall be able to shut the doors that God opens for you. May you lend unto many and borrow from none. May your barn and your storehouse be full. I pray that you will be able to pay all your debts and owe no man anything. May God open double doors for you and may you be surprised by the abundance of His blessings. As you look out for others, God will look out for you and bless you, He will multiply, keep and protect you. As you help to meet the needs of others, God will not overlook your needs. May He bless you in your going in and your coming out. May God rain His abundance upon you and your family and may you blessed in the city and in the country. May your offspring be blessed and may whatever you lay your hands on prosper. Peace be unto you now and always.

Confession:

- Lord, open to me your good treasure, the heavens. (Deut 28:12)

- Let the heavens give rain to my land in its season and bless all the work of my hand. (Deut 28:12)

- I shall lend unto many nations and borrow from none in Jesus Name. (Deut 28:12)

- I pray for the floodgates of heaven to be opened over my life. (Malachi 3:10)

- The sun shall not strike me by day nor the moon by night. (Psalm 121:6)

- The Lord will make me the head and not the tail. (Deut 28:13)

- I am above only and not beneath. (Deut 28:13)

- I am blessed in the city and blessed in the country. (Deut 28:3)

- Blessed shall be my basket and my kneading bowl. (Deut 28:5)

- Blessed shall I be when I come in, and blessed shall I be when I go out. (Deut 28:6)

- Let the heavens drop dew upon my life. (Deut 33:28)

- I bind the principalities and powers that operate against my life in Jesus Name.

- I have favour with God and with man. (Luke 2:52)

- I am blessed with all spiritual blessings in heavenly places in Christ Jesus. (Ephesians 1:3)

<u>Your verse of the day:</u>

Blessed be the God and Father of our LORD Jesus Christ, who has blessed us with every spiritual blessing In the heavenly places in Christ.

(Ephesians 1:3)

MAY YOU SING A NEW SONG TO THE LORD

SING to the LORD
A new song, for He has done
Marvelous things!
Psalm 98:1

My prayer for you today is that you will be able to sing a new song unto the Lord God your Maker, the Holy One of Israel, the Alpha and the Omega, the Beginning and the End. I pray that you will sing a new song unto our God, the Bush that is burning but never consumed. Sing unto Jehovah *Jireh*, your Provider, unto Jehovah *Nissi*, your Banner, sing unto Jehovah *Yahweh*, the Almighty. I pray you will sing and praise Him for His acts of power. Praise Him for His surpassing greatness. Praise Him in His Sanctuary and praise Him in His mighty heavens.

God is saying to you, *"My child, my beloved, I desire that you praise Me in this hour, in this time, more than you've ever done before and you will see your enemies flee before you. They shall come out against you one way and flee before you seven ways. If only you will just praise Me."*

I heard the Holy Spirit say to me that God desires His children to begin to sing a new song unto Him. He wants you to open your mouth and sing instead of complain, sing instead of moan, sing in the midst of trials, sing when you are feeling low, sing when you are feeling high, sing in spite of what you might be going through, sing, sing, sing... Sing unto the Lord a new song. When you sing to the Lord, the devil flees from you.

I pray that the Lord God will give you a new song to sing every year. May His praises never depart from your lips. In spite of what you may go through, I pray that the fruits of your lips will give Him praise.

Your singing will bring victory and deliverance into your situation. It will bring deliverance to your household; to your marriage, your children, and all that concerns you. You will be energized and refreshed by the Spirit of God. The Hosts of heaven will visit you and deliver you. Your praise will attract the God of heaven into your circumstances and all your enemies will be scattered. So, praise Him when things are tough, praise Him when times are good. Praise Him in the morning, praise Him in the daytime, and praise

Him   when   the   sun   goes   down.

The Bible says in Psalm 150:6, *"Let everything that has breath praise the Lord."* Have you got breath? Praise the Lord! Why, because praise is a weapon of war. When you sing and praise, your enemies become confused, demoralised, discouraged and disengaged. Your singing is a weapon against the enemy of your soul, Satan. The devil prefers to hear you complain and moan than to praise and worship. When you fulfill his desire by complaining and moaning, you equip him with weapons of defeat that he would then use to fight against you. When you moan and complain, the enemy becomes attracted to you. It's like an invitation, a song, the sort of confession he likes to hear. It energises the camp of the enemy. The more you complain, the more the devil is energised for attack, but when you make the choice to start singing and praising God regardless of your circumstances, the enemy becomes confused, disengaged and scattered. When you sing in the Holy Spirit, evil spirits will leave (Read 1 Samuel 16:23).

May your singing birth uncommon events in your life in Jesus name. As you sing, may your enemies be smitten before you. *"And when they began to sing and to praise, the Lord set ambushments against the children of Ammon, Moab, and Mount Seir, which were come against Judah; and they were smitten,"* (2 Chronicles 20:22 NKV)

God bless you as you walk in obedience today and sing a new song unto the Lord.

<u>Your verse of the day:</u>

Praise God in His sanctuary;

Praise Him in His mighty firmament!

Praise Him for His mighty acts;

Praise Him according to His excellent greatness!

Praise Him with the sound of the trumpet;

Praise Him with the lute and harp!
Praise Him with the timbrel and dance;

Praise Him with stringed instruments and flutes!
Praise Him with loud cymbals;

Praise Him with clashing cymbals!

Let everything that has breath praise the Lord.

Praise the Lord! (Psalm 150:1-6)

MAY YOU SOAR LIKE AN EAGLE

Those who hope in the LORD
Will renew their strength.
They will soar on wings like eagles.
Isaiah 40:31

I pray that you will see this day as a new chapter in your life. I pray that you will try and forget about what happened yesterday and soar like an eagle. An eagle continues to fly no matter what the storm might bring in its way. It rides the storm to get to the next level. I pray that the spirit of God will lift up the spirit in your inner man so that you can soar like the eagle. I pray that the cobwebs of your mind will be blown away by the Spirit of God so you can find peace. I pray that you will be able to accept yourself for who you are and accept God for who He is, a caring and loving God. He cares about you and loves you very much, so much so that He sent His one and only begotten Son to die for you and for me. May the peace of God that passes all understanding guard and guide your heart in Christ and may your day be abundantly blessed today and always.

Confession:

- I am blessed with spiritual blessings in heavenly places in Christ Jesus. (Ephesians 1:3)

- I am sitting in heavenly places in Christ Jesus. (Ephesians 2:6)

- Jesus is Lord over my spirit, my soul and my body.

- I have victory through our Lord Jesus Christ. (1 Corinthians 15:57)

- I am complete in Christ. (Colossians 2:10)

- I can do all things through Christ who strengthens me. (Philippians 4:13)

- I have the mind of Christ. (1 Corinthians 2:16)

- I am redeemed from the curse through the blood of Jesus. (Galatians 3:13)

- I am the seed of Abraham, and his blessing is mine. (Galatians 3:14)

- The enemy's flame will not kindle upon me. (Isaiah 43:2)

- I overcome every fiery trial sent against my life by the enemy in Jesus Name. (1 Peter 1:7)

- I shall not die, but live, and declare the works of the Lord. (Psalm 118:17)

- The Lord is my strength and song, and He has become my salvation. (Psalm 118:14)

- I am an overcomer; I overcome by the blood of the Lamb and by the word of my testimony.

- The Lord shall set me high upon a rock.

- God is with me, His rod and His staff they comfort me. (Psalm 23:4)

- I shall soar like an eagle in Jesus name.

Your verse of the day:

Those who wait on the LORD shall renew their strength; they shall mount up with wings like eagles, they shall run and not be weary, they shall walk and not faint. (Isaiah 40:31)

MAY YOU BE DELIVERED FROM EVIL

I pray the LORD will bless you and protect you,
And that He will show you mercy and kindness.
Numbers 6:24-36

May the Lord be good to you and give you peace.

I pray for you today that whatever may seem like a mountain before you will be turned into a plain. I pray that the problems that have become a mountain in your life will be removed and you will find solution to your problems. May all the pain you have in your heart be healed in Jesus name. May the love of God embrace and surround you. May you find joy in the midst of sorrow. May you find peace in the midst of trouble. May the hand of God uphold you in your hour of weakness and may the grace of God be sufficient for you. No evil shall befall you nor shall any plague come near your dwelling.

May today be the beginning of a victorious journey for you. May you find the grace and heart to forgive others for trespassing against you. May God bless you, bless your family, and bless your friends. May God bless you at work and in your going out and coming in. May your marriage, relationship and children be blessed. May you find hope in the midst of adversity and may God deliver you from evil today and always. Amen. This is my prayer for you. God bless you as you receive this prayer and make it yours.

Confession:

- I speak to every mountain in my life and command it to be removed and cast into the sea. (Mark 11:23)

- I command the mountains to hear the Word of the Lord and be removed in Jesus Name. (Ezekiel 36:4)

- Make waste the evil mountains in my life, O Lord. (Isaiah 42:15)

- Make darkness light before me, and crooked places straight. (Isaiah 42:16)

- I break and release myself from all curses of the enemy in Jesus Name.

- I choose blessing instead of cursing and life instead of death in Jesus Name. (Deut11:26)

- I break and rebuke all curses of sickness and infirmity in Jesus Name.

- Let those gathered against me be scattered in Jesus Name.

- No weapon formed against me shall prosper.

- I break and release myself from all spoken curses and negative words spoken against me by others in Jesus Name.

- Lord, strengthen the bars of my gates and bless my family. (Psalm 147:13)

- Lord, make peace within my borders in Jesus Name. (Psalm 147:14)

- Open before me the gates, that I may go in and receive the treasures of darkness and hidden riches of secret places in Jesus Name. (Isaiah 45:1-3)

- The gates of hell shall not prevail against me in Jesus Name. (Matthew 16:18)

Your verse of the day:

No weapon formed against you shall prosper, and every tongue which rises against you in judgment you shall condemn. This is the heritage of the servants of the LORD, and their righteousness is from Me, says the LORD.

(Isaiah 54:17)

PRAYER FOR THE JOBSEEKER

I felt led by the Lord to pray for those seeking employment and those that are looking to change jobs, and also for promotion in your current job. You may be asking God for promotion so you can earn more to pay your bills or you may not have had a job for many years now. God says I should tell you that you must not let your faith die. Perhaps the enemy is trying to erode your confidence by telling you lies that you are not good enough or that you can never succeed in life. Let me reassure you that God is willing and able. He is willing and able to provide for you and your family. He is willing and able to change your circumstance. He is the only One that can make beauty from ashes. The Lord said I should tell you that He has not lost control yet and He is in the midst of your life. He is watching over you right now and is watching over His Word to perform it in your life. God has a plan and purpose for your life that no man can alter.

I pray that God will open new doors of opportunity for you and that He will give you favour when you go for interviews. I pray that your faith will not fail and that you will not give up in spite of disappointments. I pray that the Lord will bless you and increase you on every side and that you will not fail at work. I pray that you will get financial increase and that you will be promoted and given new opportunities to grow and flourish in your job. I pray that you will find favour amongst your work colleagues and Managers. I pray that the Lord will move every obstacle out of your path and increase your faith. May God help you to be confident and give you clear direction as you perform your responsibilities at work.

If you are looking for a new job, I pray that God will open doors that will bring prosperity your way. I bind the spirit of failure at the edge of your breakthrough and I command the gates of employment to be opened to you in Jesus Name. I pray that the anointing of God will fall on you and that you will get your desired job. I pray that you will excel amongst your competitors in Jesus Name, and that you will find favour with employers. I bind the spirit of fear and intimidation that may be sent as arrows against you. I command every gate of brass in your life to be broken to pieces and every crooked path be made straight. You will be successful in Jesus Name. I cover you with the blood of Jesus and I pray that you will be satisfied with every blessing from above. You are precious, God has not given up on you, so don't give

up on yourself. Believe that all things are possible and it shall be possible for you.

<u>Your verse of the day:</u>

For I know the thoughts that I think toward you, says the LORD, thoughts of peace and not of evil, to give you a future and a hope.

(Jeremiah 29:11) NIV

PRAYER FOR YOUR MARRIAGE

A lot of marriages are going through hurt and pain and couples are being torn apart by the satanic spirit of asunder. Many are crying in silence and don't know where to turn or who to trust. If you are in great need of prayer for your marriage and your home, do not despair all is not lost.

My prayer for you today is that God will strengthen your marriage and make you secure in your home. I pray that the Lord will bring peace into your home and make your children secure. I pray that the evil spirit of household wickedness will be removed from your home in Jesus Name. I pray the Lord will be your everlasting light and your days of sorrow will end. I pray that God will bring life back into your marriage and all your enemies will be put to shame. I pray that the mighty hand of God will ignite your hearts for one another and that you will find room in your hearts to forgive each other. I pray that God will contend with those that contend with you and fight against those that fight against your marriage.

I pray if your heart is broken that God will bring healing to your heart and set you free from pain. I pray that God will deliver you from self harming and suicidal spirits and that your children and family will not mourn over you. You shall live and not die in Jesus Name. I pray that God will reach out to you and your spouse and minister deliverance to the one who has dishonoured the marriage vow. I pray that God will give you the strength to persevere and that the enemy's plans will be defeated. I plead the blood of Jesus Christ against any spirits of adultery in your marriage. I plead the blood of Jesus against spirits of miscommunication that cause you to misunderstand each other and bring arguments into your home. I pray that your spouse will respect and honour you instead of putting others above you. I pray that none of you will listen to the counsel of unfriendly friends and that God will lead you to people who will stand and pray with you. If your spouse has left home and is not willing to reconcile, I pray that God will restore your marriage and bind you both together with a cord that cannot be broken. I pray if your spouse is having an affair that the Lord will restore love and hope in your marriage and break the spirit of adultery off of your spouse's life. I pray that the Spirit of Almighty God will brood over your marriage and bring new life into your home in Jesus Mighty Name.

You are the head and not the tail, you are above only and not beneath. No weapon fashioned against your marriage shall prosper in Jesus Name. May God uphold and carry you through these very difficult times and may He be the glory and the lifter up of your head. Your expectation will not be cut off in Jesus Name. Amen.

Confession:

- I speak to every evil mountain in my marriage and my home and command it to be removed and cast into the sea in the name of Jesus. (Mark 11:23)

- Lord, lift up a standard against any flood the enemy would try to bring into my marriage and my home in Jesus name. (Isaiah 59:19)

- I bind and cast out all demons of fear and asunder in my marriage and my home.

- The LORD is my light and my salvation, I shall not be afraid. (Psalm 27:1)

- I have not been given a spirit of fear, but of power and of love and of a sound mind. (2 Tim 1:7)

- Though an army may encamp against me, my heart shall not fear. (Psalm 27:3)

- Though war may rise against me, my confidence is in the LORD. (Psalm 27:3)

- I bind all evil counsels working against my marital life in the name of Jesus.

- I release my husband/wife from the counsel of the wicked and from any demonic bondage in Jesus Name.

- I bind the spirit of marriage destruction and extra marital affairs in the name of Jesus.

- I break every yoke of marital failure in my life in the name of Jesus.

- Lord, restore my marriage and let your anointing bring abundant life, peace, joy and unity back into my home.

- Let the fire of God surround and protect my marriage, my home and my children from all destruction.

- I cancel and nullify every curse issued against my marriage and my home.

- I break all spoken curses and negative words that we have spoken over our marriage, our home and our children in the name of Jesus.

- I command all devils to leave my home in the name of Jesus.

- I am an overcomer because He who is in me is greater than he who is in the world. (1 John 4:4)

- Lord, set me in safety from them who puff at me. (Psalm 12:5)

- Let every negative influence on my home be nullified in Jesus Name.

- I shall be strong and do exploits.

FORGIVENESS

- Lord, forgive us our trespasses.

- Let us be humble enough to apologise to each other.

FOR PEACE IN THE HOME

- Lord, transform my marriage by the power of the Holy Spirit and fill my home with your peace in Jesus Name.

- You are the Prince of Peace, come and reign in my marriage and my home.

- Let peace be within my walls and prosperity within my palaces. (Psalm 122:7)

- Let my marriage be filled with your peace and my home with your joy.

- Give us strength and compassion to understand each other.

- My marriage is delivered from the power of darkness and translated into the Kingdom of God's dear Son. (Col 1:13)

- Lord, hide my marriage and my home in your pavilion, in the secret place of your tabernacle.

- Lord, set my marriage high upon a rock and deliver us from evil. (Psalm 27:5)

- Let your peace fall on our home and fill our hearts with joy.

HEALING

- Lord, heal our broken hearts and bind up our wounds. (Psalm 147:3)

- Help us to forgive each other even as Christ has forgiven us.

Your verse of the day:

The Lord is my Helper; I will not be seized with alarm,

[I will not fear or dread or be terrified].

What can man do to me?

(Ps. 27:1;118:6)

PRAYER FOR PROTECTION AND STRENGTH

Use as a prayer of personal confession for yourself for strength and divine protection.

Psalm 91

I who dwell in the secret place of the Most High

Shall abide under the shadow of the Almighty.

Today I say of the LORD, You are my refuge and my

fortress;

My God, in You I trust.

Surely You shall deliver me from the snare of the

fowler

And from the perilous pestilence.

You shall cover me with Your feathers,

And under Your wings I take refuge;

Your truth *shall be my* shield and buckler.

I shall not be afraid of the terror by night,

Nor of the arrow *that* flies by day,

Nor of the pestilence *that* walks in darkness,

Nor of the destruction *that* lays waste at noonday.

A thousand may fall at my side,

And ten thousand at my right hand;

But it shall not come near me.

Only with my eyes shall I look,

And see the reward of the wicked.

Because I have made the LORD, *who is* my refuge,

Even the Most High, my dwelling place,

No evil shall befall me

Nor shall any plague come near my dwelling;

For the Lord shall give His angels charge over me,

To keep me in all my ways.

In *their* hands they shall bear me up,

Lest I dash my foot against a stone.

I shall tread upon the lion and the cobra,

The young lion and the serpent I shall trample

underfoot.

Because I have set my love upon the Lord therefore He

will deliver me;

The Lord will set me on high, because I have known

His name.

I shall call upon the Lord, and He will answer me;

He *will be* with me in trouble;

He will deliver me and honor me.

With long life will He satisfy me,

And show me His salvation.

THE LORD IS YOUR SHEPHERD

Use as a prayer of personal confession for yourself for God's care and provision.

<u>Psalm 23</u>

The LORD *is* my shepherd;

I shall not want.

He makes me to lie down in green pastures;

He leads me beside the still waters.

He restores my soul;

He leads me in the paths of righteousness

For His name's sake.

Yea, though I walk through the valley of the shadow of death,

I will fear no evil;

For You *are* with me;

Your rod and Your staff, they comfort me.

You prepare a table before me in the presence of my enemies;

You anoint my head with oil;

My cup runs over.

Surely goodness and mercy shall follow me

All the days of my life;

And I will dwell in the house of the LORD

Forever. Amen.

A PRAYER OF PEACE

Use as a prayer of personal confession for yourself for peace when your heart is troubled.

- You are a shield around me, O LORD; you bestow glory on me and lift up my head. (Psalm 3:3).

- Let the peace of God guard my heart and mind in Christ Jesus. (Philippians 4:7).

- Peace of Christ be a shield around me.

- The Lord is my shepherd I shall not want. He makes me lie down in green pastures; he leads me beside still waters. He restores my soul. (Psalm 23:1-3)

- Father, into your hands I commit my concerns, my worries, my anxieties and I cast all my cares on you because you care for me.

- I will not be anxious or worry, I will be still before the LORD and wait patiently for Him; I will not fret. (Psalm 37:7)

- My soul finds rest in God alone. He only is my rock and my salvation; He is my defense; I shall not be greatly moved. (Psalm 62:1-2)

- Be at rest once more, O my soul... (Psalm 116:7).

"Let the peace of Christ rule in my heart" (Colossians 3:15).

Peace of Christ rule in my heart, guard my heart and mind in Christ Jesus.

PRAYER IN TIMES OF DISAPPOINTMENT

<u>Psalm46</u>

God *is* my refuge and my strength,

A very present help in times of trouble.

Therefore **I will not fear**,

Even though the earth be removed,

And though the mountains be carried into the midst of

the sea;

Though its waters roar *and* be troubled,

Though the mountains shake with its swelling.

There is a river whose streams shall make glad the city

of God,

The holy *place* of the tabernacle of the Most High.

God *is* in the midst of my life, I shall not be moved;

God shall help me, just at the break of dawn.

The nations raged, the kingdoms were moved;

He uttered His voice, the earth melted.

The LORD of hosts *is* with me;

The God of Jacob *is* my refuge.

Come, behold the works of the LORD,

Who has made desolations in the earth.

He makes wars cease to the end of the earth;

He breaks the bow and cuts the spear in two;

He burns the chariot in the fire.

Be still, and know that I *am* God;
I will be exalted among the nations,
I will be exalted in the earth!

The LORD of hosts *is* with me;
The God of Jacob *is* my refuge.

**Take some time to meditate on these words,
imagine yourself in God's care and repeat the
following verses several times:**

"God is my refuge and strength,
A very present help in times of trouble.
Therefore I will not fear,

God is in the midst of my life, I shall not be moved;
God shall help me, just at the break of dawn.

The LORD of hosts is with me;
The God of Jacob is my refuge."

The LORD of hosts is with me;
The God of Jacob is my refuge.

STEPS TO PEACE WITH GOD

God loves you and wants you to experience peace in this life and in the life to come. The Bible says we can only have peace through our Lord Jesus Christ.

"We have peace with God through our Lord Jesus Christ." (Romans 5:1)

We can only experience peace, abundance and eternal life through our Lord Jesus Christ, so I would like to gently encourage you that if you do not know Jesus Christ as your Lord and Saviour, please confess the prayer below. God bless you as do so.

PRAYER

How to Pray:

Dear Lord Jesus, I know that I am a sinner, and I ask for Your forgiveness. I believe You died for my sins and rose from the dead. I turn from my sins and invite You to come into my heart and life. I want to trust and follow You as my Lord and Saviour. In Your Name. Amen.

God's Assurance is His Word

If you prayed this prayer, the Bible says ...

"Everyone who calls on the name of the Lord will be saved."

—*Romans 10:13*

May the peace of our Lord Jesus Christ abide with you now and forever... Amen.

BIBLE VERSES ABOUT PEACE

"Peace I leave with you, My peace I give to you; not as the world gives do I give to you. Let not your heart be troubled, neither let it be afraid." (John 14:27)

These *things I have spoken to you, that in Me you may have peace. In the world you will have tribulation; but be of good cheer, I have overcome the world." (John 16:33)*

Be anxious for nothing, but in everything by prayer and supplication, with thanksgiving, let your requests be made known to God; ⁷ and the peace of God, which surpasses all understanding, will guard your hearts and minds through Christ Jesus. (Philippians 4:6-7)

And let the peace of God rule in your hearts, to which also you were called in one body; and be thankful. (Colossians 3:15)

For God is not the author of confusion but of peace, as in all the churches of the saints. (1 Corinthians 14:33)

Come to Me, all you who labour and are heavy laden, and I will give you rest. Take My yoke upon you and learn from Me, for I am gentle and lowly in heart, and you will find rest for your souls. For My yoke is easy and My burden is light." (Matthew 11:28-30)

Now may the Lord of peace Himself give you peace always in every way. The Lord be with you all. *(2 Thessalonians 3:16)*

ABOUT THE AUTHOR

Freda Lade-Ajumobi was born in Manchester, England. She was brought up in a Christian home with God fearing, loving and dedicated parents.

She is a graduate of Art and Design and attended the History Maker's Bible School at the Emmanuel Centre, Victoria, London.

She is an anointed Minister, a gifted and dynamic speaker and teacher of the word of God. A prayer warrior and an intercessor with a passion to serve and minister to people. She has been serving the body of Christ for over 20 years and gave her life to Christ in 1984.

Her calling and anointing is in the area of the prophetic, encouragement and teaching of the Word and has enriched many lives with this gift. She is the founder of Unique Ministries, a ministry that is fulfilling the call of God on her life, to teach, preach, inspire, encourage and minister to the body of Christ across all denominations.

She is married to Afolabi and they are blessed with a lovely son, Timi.

She loves the Lord with all her heart and desires above all to spread the knowledge of God's glory to the uttermost ends of the earth through her books, Internet blogs, paintings and ministering the Word of God to a hurt and broken world.

Printed in Great Britain
by Amazon

87235129R00077